Sports Illustrated KIDS

GAME DAY

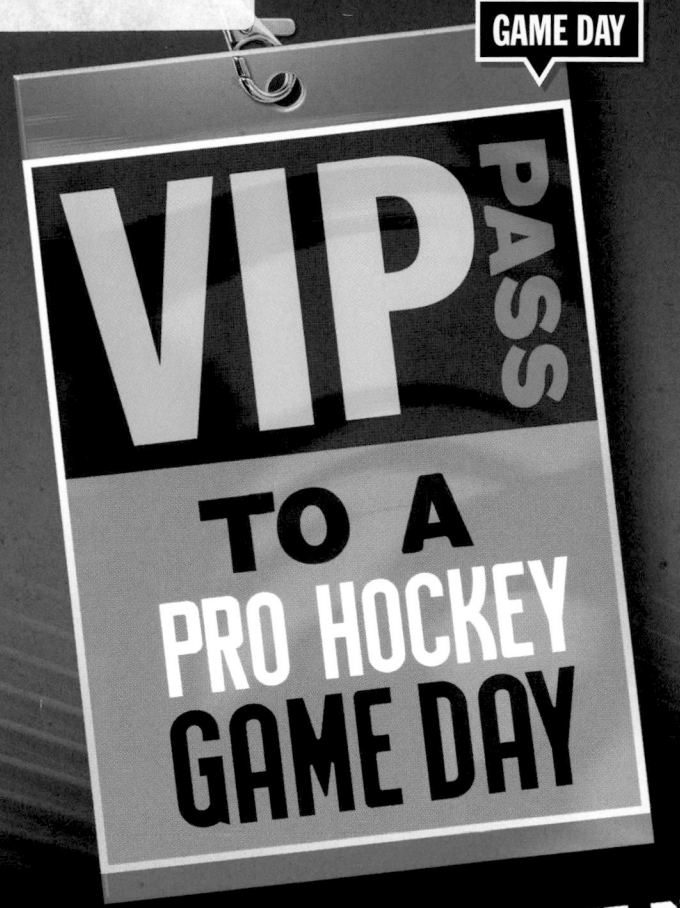

VIP PASS

TO A
PRO HOCKEY
GAME DAY

FROM THE LOCKER ROOM TO THE PRESS BOX
[AND EVERYTHING IN BETWEEN]

by Clay Latimer

Consultant:
Joe Schmit
Sports Director, KSTP-TV
St. Paul, Minnesota

CAPSTONE PRESS
a capstone imprint

Sports Illustrated KIDS Game Day is published by Capstone Press,
151 Good Counsel Drive, P.O. Box 669, Mankato, Minnesota 56002.
www.capstonepub.com

Books published by Capstone Press are manufactured with paper
containing at least 10 percent post-consumer waste.

Library of Congress Cataloging-in-Publication Data
Latimer, Clay, 1952–
    VIP pass to a pro hockey game day: from the locker room to the press box
    (and everything in between) / by Clay Latimer.
    p. cm.—(Sports Illustrated KIDS. Game day.)
    Includes bibliographical references and index.
    Summary: "Describes various activities and people who work behind the
scenes during a National Hockey League game"—Provided by publisher.
    ISBN 978-1-4296-5464-7 (library binding)
    ISBN 978-1-4296-6286-4 (paperback)
1. Hockey—Juvenile literature. 2. National Hockey League—Juvenile
literature. I. Title.
GV847.25.L38 2011
796.962—dc22   2010032211

Editorial Credits
Aaron Sautter, editor; Ted Williams, designer; Eric Gohl,
    media researcher; Eric Manske, production specialist

Photo Credits
Getty Images Inc./Jeff Vinnick, 6; NHLI/Andy Devlin, 16; NHLI/Dave
    Reginek, 20; NHLI/Jeff Vinnick, 13; NHLI/Len Redkoles, 29
iStockphoto/Nicole Waring, background (hockey ice)
Newscom/Icon SMI 740/Shelly Castellano, 25
Sports Illustrated/Damian Strohmeyer, 26, 28; David E. Klutho, cover,
    4, 8, 14, 19, 22, 23, 27; Robert Beck, 9, 10, 11

Design Elements
Shutterstock/bioraven; Daniela Illing; Iwona Grodzka;
    Marilyn Volan; Zavodskov Anatoliy Nikolaevich

Printed in the United States of America in Stevens Point, Wisconsin.

092010   005934WZS11

TABLE OF CONTENTS

[ACTION BEYOND THE RINK]

A National Hockey League (NHL) game is jam-packed with dramatic moments. But the excitement doesn't just happen on the ice. Behind every successful power play is a hardworking coach. Entertainment crews keep crowds amused with scoreboard videos. And every road trip requires a small army of equipment staff.

Power plays, penalties, and slap shots are only part of game day. Every game involves a lot of action the fans never see. What do referees do to prepare for each game? How do players pass the time during a cross-country flight? What do newspaper reporters do before a game? Turn the page to discover all the work that goes into a professional hockey game.

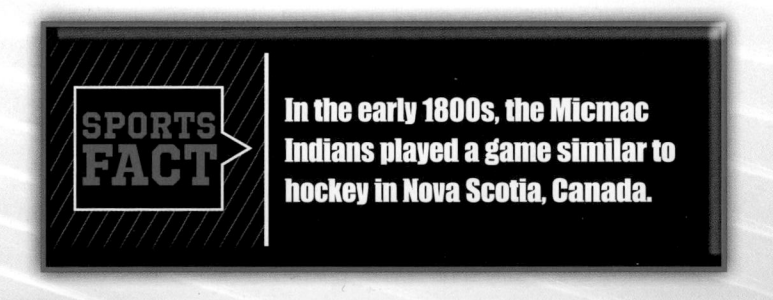

SPORTS FACT

In the early 1800s, the Micmac Indians played a game similar to hockey in Nova Scotia, Canada.

ON THE ROAD AGAIN

The road seems like an endless grind for NHL players. They often travel in the dead of winter to North America's coldest cities. One day blends into another. A 10-day road trip becomes a blur of early wake-up calls, blizzards, and icy streets.

Players relax in large, comfortable seats during long flights between games.

But at least the team travels in comfort. Players and coaches travel on private jets and comfortable buses. To pass the time, players watch movies, listen to music, or play cards. Meanwhile, the coaching staff prepares the game plan. Soon the team is served steak, pasta, and other fine foods. Plenty of ice cream, cookies, and cake are provided for dessert.

When the players arrive at a new city, a bus takes them to a fancy hotel. Bellhops carry the players' luggage to large, comfortable rooms. Getting plenty of sleep helps players do their best on game day. And after a long day of travel, the team is sure to sleep well.

■ AN EXHAUSTING JOURNEY

In 1905 the Dawson City Klondikers journeyed 4,400 miles (7,081 kilometers) to play the Ottawa Senators for the Stanley Cup. The squad began its trip in the Yukon Territory in Canada. They traveled 46 miles (74 km) by dogsled the first day and 41 miles (66 km) the next. After waiting five days, they took a boat to Seattle, Washington. Then they rode on several trains to get to Ottawa, Ontario. After 23 days of travel, the Klondikers finally arrived at their destination. However, the team was exhausted after such a long trip. They were no match for the Senators and lost the series.

WAKE-UP CALL

A player rolls out of bed early on a freezing January morning. Still tired and sleepy, he dresses, grabs a bite to eat, and heads out the door. Another day is dawning in the NHL. For tired hockey players, it means one thing—it's time for the morning skate.

Coaches and players run through the game plan and practice plays at the morning skate.

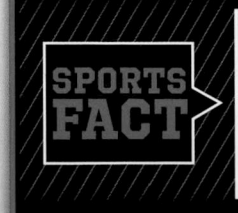

SPORTS FACT The NHL's Stanley Cup is the oldest prize in North American sports. It has been awarded each year since 1893, except in 1919. A flu outbreak caused the competition to be canceled that year.

Players often use free time to relax in their hotel rooms before the game.

The morning skate is a light practice that takes place early on game day. The home team goes first, followed by the visiting squad. Before hitting the ice, each team meets in its locker room. The players listen as the coach outlines the game plan. Then they stretch, strap on their equipment, and head to the ice. For the next hour they run through plays and work up the first sweat of the day.

Players then get the afternoon off. Some visit local schools or help out charities. Others gather for lunch at a nearby restaurant. It's a relaxed time when players can call family, friends, or agents. Then they head back to the hotel. Until game time, players relax by listening to music, watching TV, or taking a nap.

THE FINAL COUNTDOWN

Equipment staff members make sure the players' skates are sharpened before the game begins.

Tension and stress builds as game time nears. Inside the locker room, the team quickly focuses on business. The equipment staff sharpens the players' skates and lays out their uniforms. Meanwhile, the coaches meet to discuss strategy and make any last-minute adjustments.

The head coach then leads his staff into the locker room where the players are waiting. The team reviews the game plan and watches game film of its opponent. They want to be as prepared as possible before hitting the ice.

As the minutes tick down, the pace picks up. A trainer leads the players through some stretching exercises. Then they file out of the locker room and down a long hallway. As fans settle into their seats, the teams skate onto the ice for their final pre-game warm-ups.

■ EQUIPPING THE TEAM

Equipment staff do about 80 loads of laundry a week. They wash everything from towels to practice jerseys. They make sure the team's skates, sticks, helmets, and pads are in good shape for each game. Equipment managers are also responsible for supplying the team with hockey pucks. A team can use up to 3,000 game pucks and 10,000 practice pucks in a season.

ICE SHOW

In the NHL, hockey and fun go hand in hand. Fans stand and yell. They stomp their feet. They boo opposing players. But it doesn't end there. To entertain fans, entertainment crews put on a big show. Loudspeakers blare rock music. Highlight videos flash across huge scoreboard screens. Mini blimps soar above the crowd and drop **souvenirs**. Something is always happening.

Putting on a fun show for fans is hard work. Entertainment crews meet three hours before the game. Directors decide on the music and video clips and hand out instructions to their staff. During the game, they wear headsets to direct their assistants. They make sure the fans keep having fun, even during breaks in the action.

souvenir—an object kept as a reminder of the game

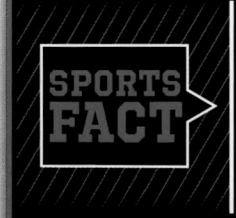

SPORTS FACT

The Calgary Flames' mascot Harvey the Hound received a big surprise in 2003. While performing behind the opponent's bench, he angered Edmonton coach Craig MacTavish. The Oilers' coach ripped the tongue right out of the canine's furry mouth!

Entertainment crews keep track of the action behind the scenes.

Between each period of play, fans like to shop for T-shirts, caps, and pucks with the team's logo. They gobble up pizza, hot dogs, and drinks while talking about the game. Meanwhile, cheerleaders perform routines on the ice, and the team mascot mingles with the crowd. It all adds up to a fun time for everyone.

MAKING THE CALL

They are often booed and criticized. Some have been knocked unconscious by pucks. Others have had bones shattered by slap shots. But night after night they come back, ready for another game. They're NHL officials.

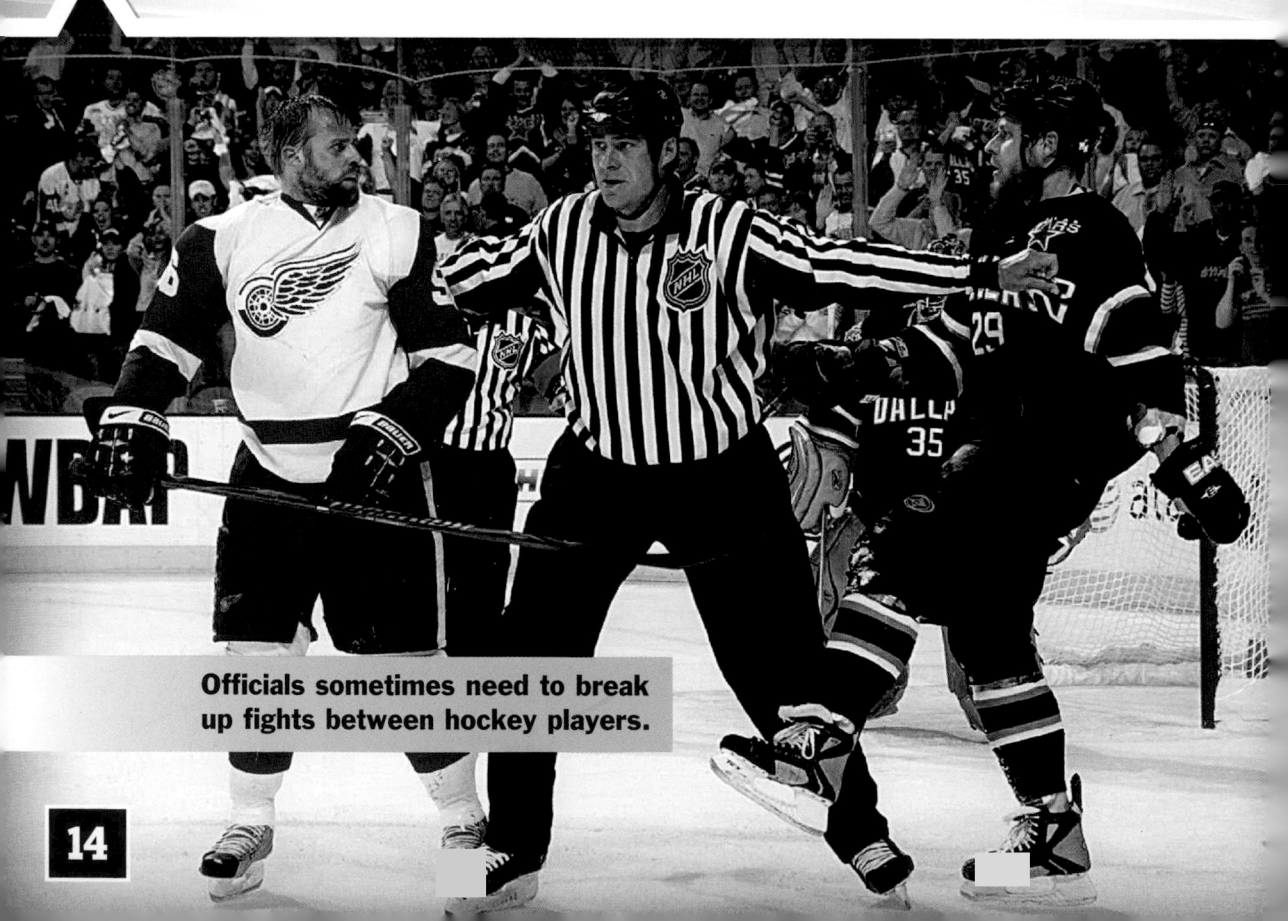

Officials sometimes need to break up fights between hockey players.

Before the game begins, the officials warm up with some stretching exercises. Then they review each team's lineup. During the game, officials try to blend into the action and avoid being noticed by the fans. The best officials know that the only time they should be seen is when a **penalty** is called.

Arguments between teams can quickly rise to a boiling point. When fights break out, the officials watch for illegal actions. Eye gouging, hair pulling, and spitting are a few things that aren't allowed. Rules about fighting take up seven pages of the NHL rulebook, and officials need to know them all.

After the game, the officiating crew reviews its performance. Did they miss a call? What would they do next time? Finally, they file an official report with the NHL.

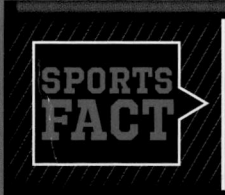

REAL

penalty—punishment of a player for breaking the rules

SPORTS FACT The NHL often struggles to find enough referees for games. In 2010 the league looked outside the United States and hired its first European referee.

HOCKEY JAIL

Penalty box officials keep track of players' penalty minutes.

Hockey players who commit penalties get sent to a **penalty box**. Some jokingly call it hockey jail. Every NHL arena has a penalty box for each team. In most arenas, glass separates the home and visiting teams' penalty boxes. In arenas without glass, the penalized players sometimes get into arguments.

penalty box—the area where penalized players serve their penalty time

Sometimes players are raging mad when they get in the box. They swing their sticks and slam doors. But most players control their emotions and focus on the action on the ice. A few players may talk with the officials about their penalties. As a player's penalty time winds down, a penalty box official counts down the final seconds. Then he swings open the door to let the player rejoin the game.

Game pucks are also kept in the penalty box. As the game proceeds, penalty box officials provide referees with new pucks. The pucks are often kept in a freezer. Keeping pucks frozen helps them glide better on the ice. Penalty box officials also hold onto any dropped sticks that referees hand them.

■ ONE BAD ATTITUDE

New York Ranger Sean Avery is known for his bad temper. He's often made offensive comments about other players and has been in many fights. Because of his bad attitude, Avery knows a thing or two about the penalty box. During a 2009 playoff game, he actually spent more time in the penalty box than he did on the ice!

ON AGAIN, OFF AGAIN

In most major sports, players don't jump in and out of games in the middle of the action. But in hockey, players constantly enter and leave games. In fact, teams make **line changes** about every 40 seconds. Coaches make line changes based on the game situation. For example, a line change might be made for a power play or to defend a lead. Coaches may also make a line change if the players on the ice become tired.

line change—when an entire line is replaced on the ice with rested players

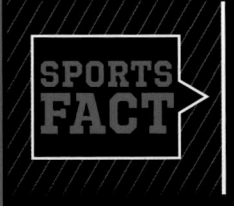

SPORTS FACT Players' sticks are organized in a rack near the bench. The names and jersey numbers of the players are marked on the sticks. This set-up helps players quickly grab their sticks and get onto the ice.

Players sit next to their fellow linemen so they can enter the game together. When the coach calls for a line change, each player calls out the name of the person he is replacing. One group rushes off the ice through a gate while the other vaults over the boards.

Coaches often use line changes as a strategy to confuse the opposing team. Players need to pay attention to line changes. If they miss an assignment, it could result in a costly penalty or even a game-changing goal.

Players jump over the boards when the coach calls for a line change.

TAKING A BREATHER

The players are exhausted after a fast-paced period of play. During the 15-minute **intermissions**, the locker room is only slightly slower-paced. Every second counts. Players chug energy drinks and loosen their skates. Trainers re-tape players' ankles and tend to cuts and bruises. Equipment staff replace broken sticks and sharpen skates.

> **intermission**—a 15-minute recess between each period of play

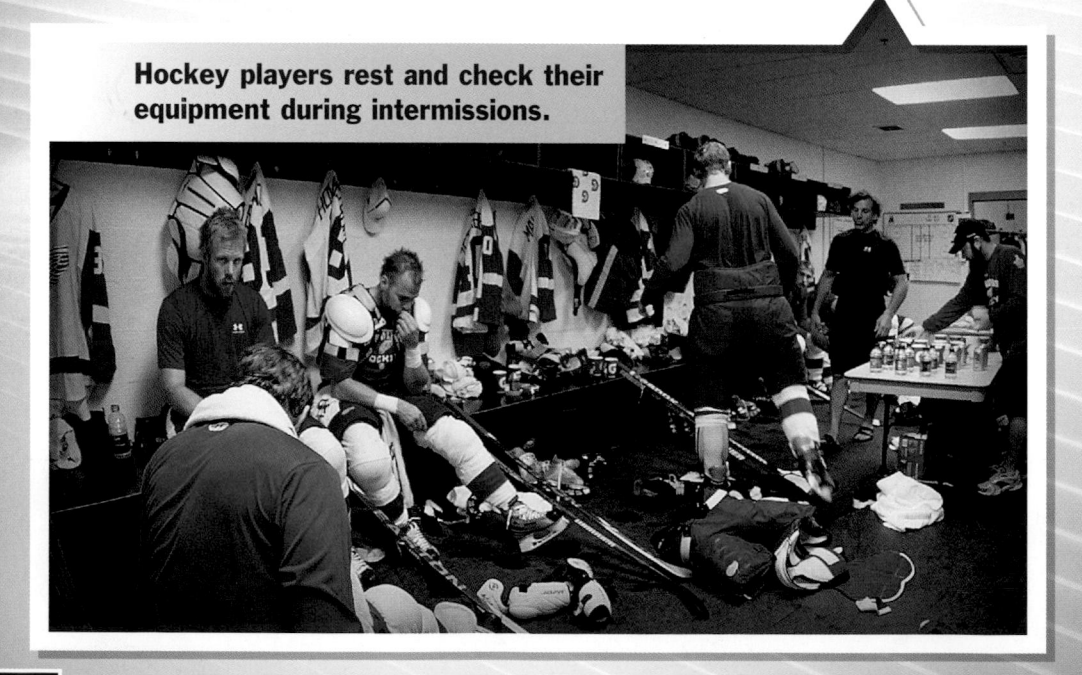

Hockey players rest and check their equipment during intermissions.

Meanwhile, coaches identify what went right or wrong in the previous period. Teams often make adjustments during a game. But for coaches, intermission is a chance to rethink strategy. They might look for ways to move the puck faster on offense. Or they might decide to focus on tightening up the defense. With five minutes left, the head coach leads his staff to the dressing room. After going over the adjustments with the team, it's time to go back to battle on the ice.

■ FUN TO WATCH, FUN TO SAY

It looks like a tank. It sounds like a huge vacuum cleaner. And it travels at only 10 miles (16 km) per hour. But it's a highlight of the game for many fans. It's the Zamboni machine—the odd-looking vehicle that makes the ice as smooth as a gleaming mirror. Two Zambonis are used to clean the ice during intermissions in each NHL game. They are often painted bright colors and decorated with advertisements. A few are even decorated to look like racecars or other vehicles. Fans often enter contests hoping to get a ride on the popular vehicle.

TENDING TO THE WOUNDED

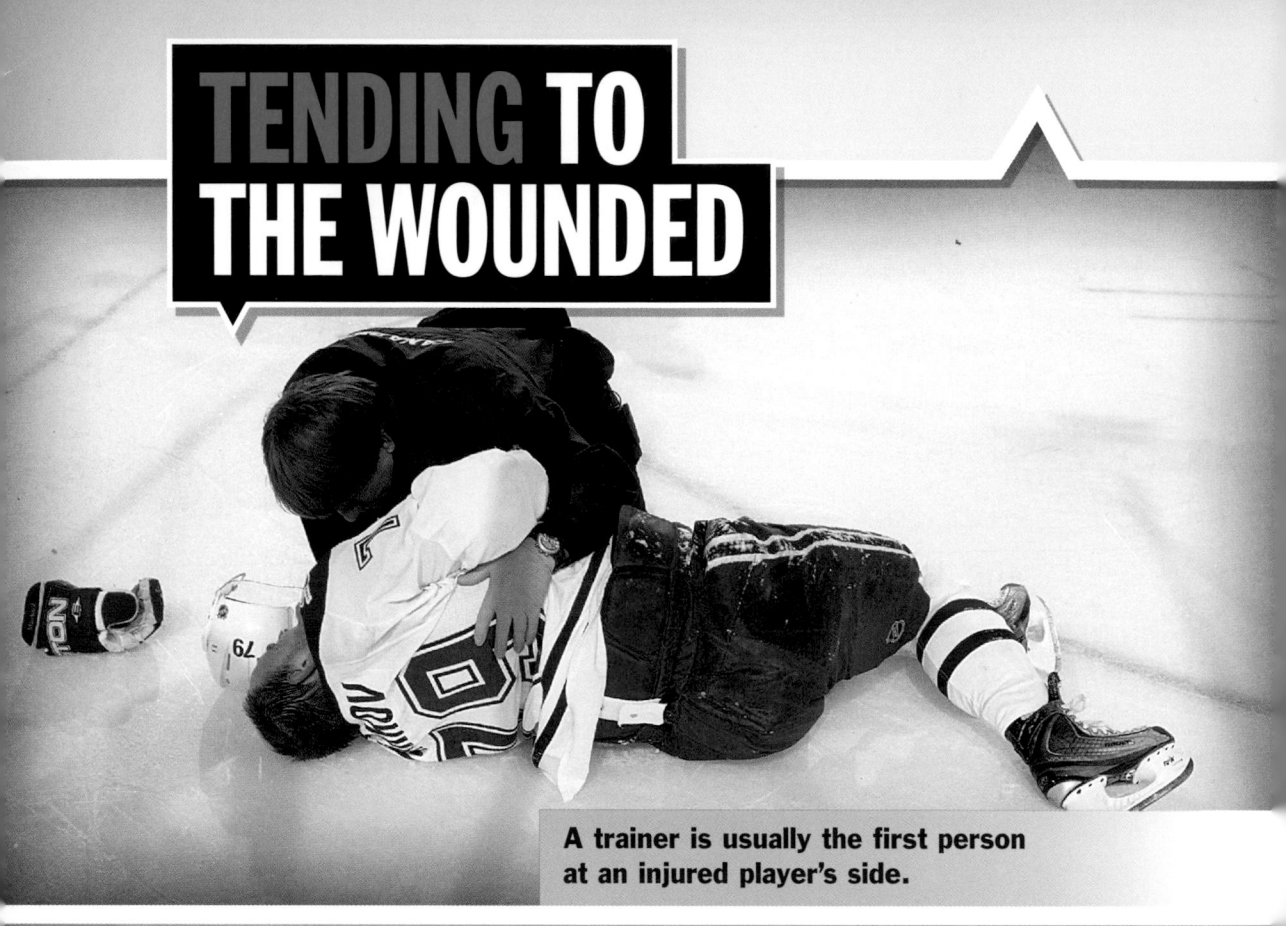

A trainer is usually the first person at an injured player's side.

A flying puck knocks out a player's tooth. Another player is carted off the ice after a brutal **body check**. A stick gashes someone's face by accident. Pro hockey players skate fast and shoot rock-hard pucks at more than 100 miles (161 km) per hour. There's no way around it—hockey is a violent sport.

body check—when a player slams into an opponent to block his progress

The team's medical staff works hard to prevent and treat injuries. Each team has a staff of doctors, dentists, trainers, a massage therapist, and a strength and conditioning coach. During each game, a team doctor and dentist sit in the stands just above the bench. If there's a serious injury, they spring into action to tend to the injured player.

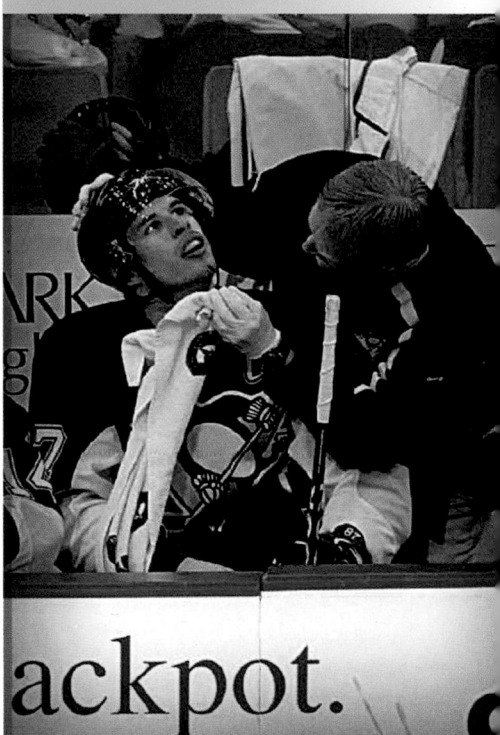

Players often need stitches for cuts and gashes they suffer in the game.

▪ ONE TOUGH PLAYER

Philadelphia Flyer Ian Laperriere once took a hard shot to his face. The puck gashed his face and knocked out several teeth. Yet Laperriere returned to the game thanks to quick work by the team's dentist, Guy Lanzi. Lanzi removed Laperriere's loose teeth and sewed in about 100 stitches. By the third period, Laperriere was back on the ice.

READ ALL ABOUT IT

High above the ice, broadcasters and reporters watch and analyze the action. Their work began hours before the game. Newspaper reporters often attend the morning skate. They like to interview players to write their first **blog** of the day. Two hours before game time, TV and radio crews arrive at the arena. The broadcasters interview players and record segments to be used for the evening news.

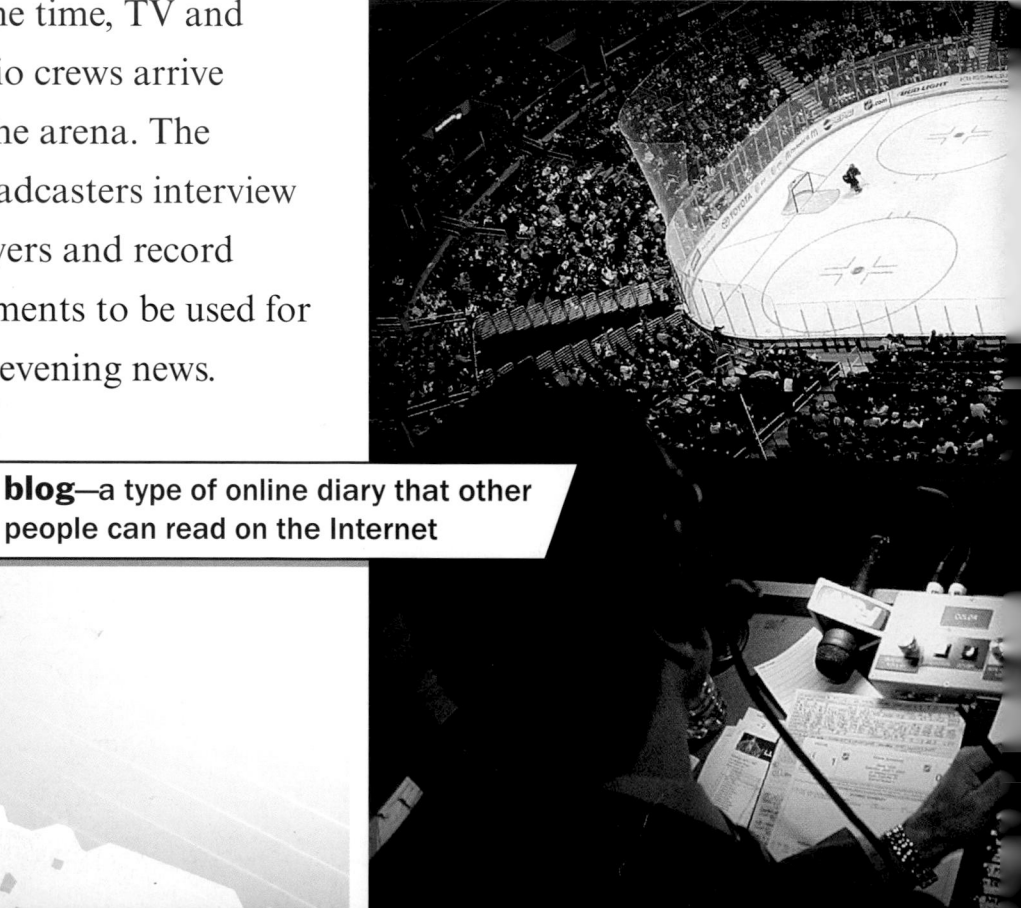

blog—a type of online diary that other people can read on the Internet

Shortly before the opening **face-off**, media members climb upstairs to press row. As the game begins, TV and radio announcers describe the action for fans at home. Color analysts explain what happens during big plays. They try to help people understand the strategies the coaches are using. Between periods, reporters catch up with players for brief interviews outside the locker room.

face-off—when an official drops the puck between two opposing players

Reporters and broadcasters watch the game action from high above the rink.

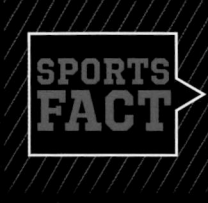

SPORTS FACT ▶ The U.S. and Canadian men's hockey teams played each other for the 2010 Olympic gold medal. The game was the most-watched TV broadcast in Canadian history.

During the game, newspaper reporters jot down notes on crucial plays and post blogs for the paper's Web site. But their main job is to write the game story. After the final buzzer, they rush to the locker rooms to interview players and coaches. They need to put the finishing touches on their stories to make the deadline for tomorrow's paper.

TV crews use several cameras to capture all the action at a game.

TURN OUT THE LIGHTS

Teams show good sportsmanship by shaking their opponents' hands.

The final horn sounds, opposing players shake hands, and another game winds down. Fans relive the game's high and low points as they stream out to their cars. High above the ice, the entertainment crew packs up its gear. In the locker rooms, reporters flock to interview key players. Equipment staff members pick up sweat-soaked jerseys and pads. Trainers tend to players' injuries. In their office, coaches begin reviewing their team's performance.

The teams soon make their way out of the arena, which is suddenly quiet and dark. But in two nights it will be loud and bright again for another NHL game. Fans, referees, and reporters will all be back for more behind-the-scenes drama.

Reporters swarm star players to get their thoughts about the game.

GLOSSARY

blog (BLOG)—a type of online diary that other people can read on the Internet

body check (BOD-ee CHEK)—when a hockey player bumps or slams into an opponent to block his progress or throw him off balance

face-off (FAYSS-awf)—when an official drops the puck between the sticks of two opposing players who try to gain control of it

intermission (in-tur-MISH-uhn)—a 15-minute recess between each period of play

line change (LINE CHAYNJ)—when an entire offensive or defensive line is changed

penalty (PEN-uhl-tee)—punishment of a player or team for breaking the rules; hockey players are punished by being removed from the game for a period of time

penalty box (PEN-uhl-tee BOKS)—an area with a bench to the side of a hockey rink where penalized players serve their penalty time

souvenir (soo-vuh-NIHR)—an object kept as a reminder of a person, place, or event

READ MORE

McClellan, Ray. *Hockey.* Minneapolis, Minn.: Bellwether Media, 2010.

Leonetti, Mike. *Hockey Now!* Buffalo, N.Y.: Firefly Books, 2008.

Thomas, Keltie. *Inside Hockey! The Legends, Facts and Feats That Made the Game.* Toronto: Maple Tree Press, 2008.

INTERNET SITES

FactHound offers a safe, fun way to find Internet sites related to this book. All of the sites on FactHound have been researched by our staff.

Here's all you do:

Visit *www.facthound.com*

Type in this code: 9781429654647

 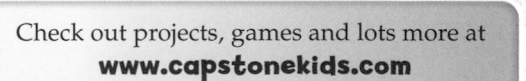

Check out projects, games and lots more at **www.capstonekids.com**

INDEX